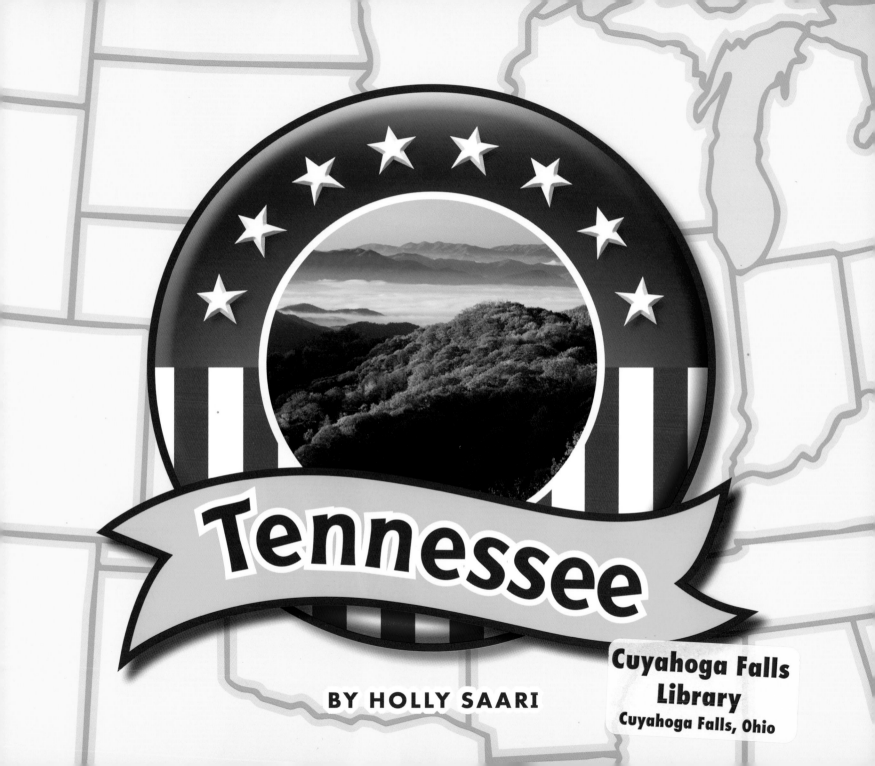

Tennessee

BY HOLLY SAARI

Published by The Child's World®
1980 Lookout Drive • Mankato, MN 56003-1705
800-599-READ • www.childsworld.com

ACKNOWLEDGMENTS
The Child's World®: Mary Berendes, Publishing Director
The Design Lab: Design and production
Red Line Editorial: Editorial direction

PHOTO CREDITS: Geir-Olav Lyngfjell/iStockphoto, cover, 1, 3; Matt Kania/
Map Hero, Inc., 4, 5; Jim Jurica/iStockphoto, 7; David Rose/iStockphoto,
9; iStockphoto, 10; Kimberly McBride/iStockphoto, 11; Jeff Greenberg/
Photolibrary, 13; The Print Collector/Photolibrary, 15; Curtis Hilbun/AP
Images, 17; Matt Sayles/AP Images, 19; Jeremy Edwards/iStockphoto, 21;
One Mile Up, 22; Quarter-dollar coin image from the United States Mint, 22

LIBRARY OF CONGRESS CATALOGING-IN-PUBLICATION DATA
Saari, Holly.
  Tennessee / by Holly Saari.
    p. cm.
  Includes bibliographical references and index.
  ISBN 978-1-60253-487-2 (library bound : alk. paper)
  1. Tennessee—Juvenile literature. I. Title.

F436.3.S23 2010
976.8—dc22

                            2010019327

Printed in the United States of America in Mankato, Minnesota.
July 2010
F11538

On the cover:
Great Smoky
Mountains
National Park
has trees that
turn beautiful
colors in the fall.

CONTENTS

Geography

Let's explore Tennessee! Tennessee is in the southeastern part of the United States. The Mississippi River is Tennessee's western border.

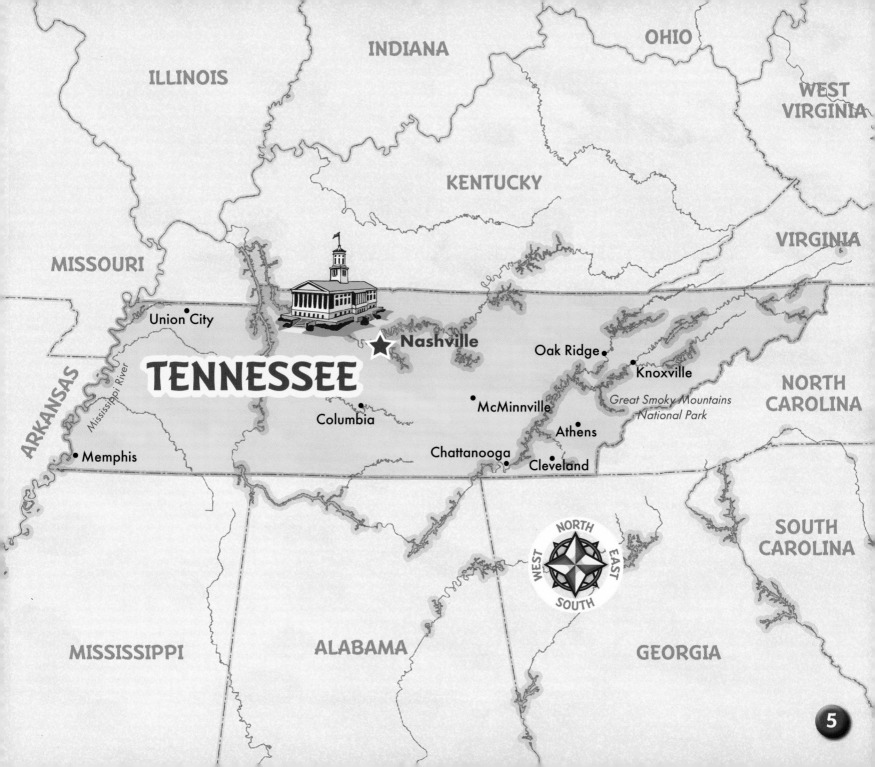

ILLINOIS

INDIANA

OHIO

MISSOURI

KENTUCKY

WEST VIRGINIA

VIRGINIA

Union City

NORTH CAROLINA

TENNESSEE

Mississippi River

Nashville

Oak Ridge

Knoxville

McMinnville

Columbia

Great Smoky Mountains National Park

Athens

Memphis

Chattanooga

Cleveland

ARKANSAS

SOUTH CAROLINA

NORTH

WEST   EAST

SOUTH

MISSISSIPPI

ALABAMA

GEORGIA

Cities

Nashville is the capital city of Tennessee. Memphis is the largest city in the state. Chattanooga and Knoxville are other well-known cities.

Memphis is on the banks of the Mississippi River. ▶

Land

Tennessee has mountains, forests, **valleys**, and rivers. The Great Smoky Mountains are in the east. Valleys are in the middle of the state. The west is flatter and has more farmland. This flat land extends to the Mississippi River.

The Tennessee River **Gorge** is near Chattanooga, Tennessee. ▶

Plants and Animals

About half of Tennessee is covered in forests. The state tree is the tulip poplar. The state flower is the iris. It often has purple **petals**. Deer, bears, and beavers live in Tennessee. The state bird is the mockingbird. It can copy the sounds of other birds.

The iris can come in many different colors, but it is often purple. ▶

People and Work

About 6.2 million people live in Tennessee. Most live in large cities. About one-third of the people live in smaller towns. Some people work in health care or stores. Other people work in **manufacturing** jobs. They make things such as food, car **equipment**, and medicine. Farmers in Tennessee raise cattle and chickens. Other people work in mining.

Apples are an important fruit crop in Tennessee. ▶

History

Native Americans have lived in this area for thousands of years. People from Europe came to the area in the 1700s. Tennessee became the sixteenth state on June 1, 1796. Many battles were fought here during the U.S. **Civil War**.

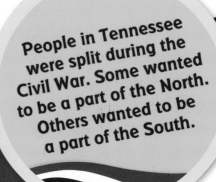

People in Tennessee were split during the Civil War. Some wanted to be a part of the North. Others wanted to be a part of the South.

Many soldiers from Tennessee lost their lives during the Civil War. ▶

Ways of Life

Tennessee is a center for music. Country and **bluegrass** are **popular** here. The state also has a strong **military** history. People visit places where Civil War battles were fought. Many people hunt and fish in Tennessee, too.

The Country Music Hall of Fame and **Museum** is in Nashville, Tennessee. ▶

Famous People

Singers Dolly Parton and Miley Cyrus were born in Tennessee. Davy Crockett was born here, too. He explored the American **frontier** in the early 1800s.

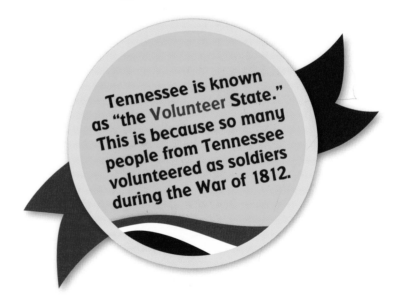

Tennessee is known as "the Volunteer State." This is because so many people from Tennessee volunteered as soldiers during the War of 1812.

Miley Cyrus is known for starring as "Hannah Montana" on the Disney Channel. ▶

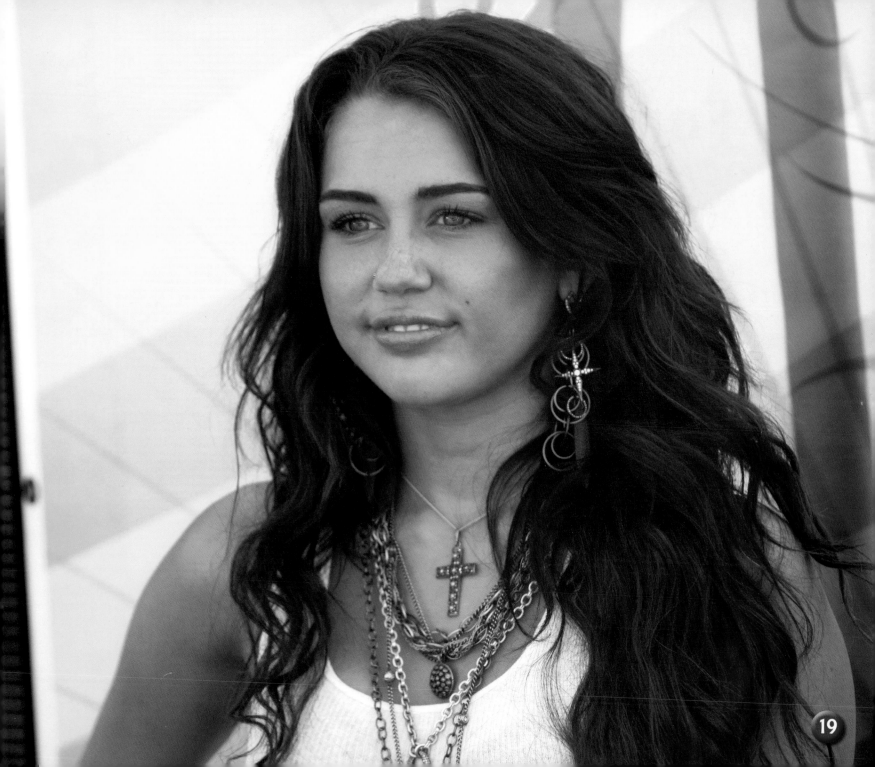

Famous Places

The Grand Ole Opry is in Nashville. This is a popular place for country music. Great Smoky Mountains National Park is another famous place. Visitors can see many animals here.

Graceland in Memphis is popular to visit. It is the former home of singer Elvis Presley.

Visitors to Great Smoky Mountains National Park can camp, fish, ride horses, and see waterfalls and wildflowers. ▶

State Symbols

Seal

Tennessee's state seal has plants and tools. They stand for farming. The seal also has a boat. This stands for business. Go to childsworld.com/links for a link to Tennessee's state Web site, where you can get a firsthand look at the state seal.

Flag

In the middle of Tennessee's mostly red flag are three white stars in a blue circle. The stars represent east, middle, and west Tennessee.

Quarter

Tennessee's state quarter shows musical instruments. The quarter came out 2002.

Glossary

bluegrass (BLOO-grass): Bluegrass is country music played on instruments such as fiddles and banjos. Bluegrass is popular in Tennessee.

Civil War (SIV-il WOR): In the United States, the Civil War was a war fought between the Northern and the Southern states from 1861 to 1865. Some Civil War battles were fought in Tennessee.

equipment (ih-KWIP-munt): Equipment is the set of items needed to do something. Some people in Tennessee make car equipment.

frontier (frun-TEER): A frontier is the edge of an area that has not yet been explored. Davy Crockett from Tennessee explored the American frontier.

gorge (GORJ): A gorge is a steep, narrow canyon. The Tennessee River Gorge is near Chattanooga.

manufacturing (man-yuh-FAK-chur-ing): Manufacturing is the task of making items with machines. Some people in Tennessee work in manufacturing.

military (MIL-uh-tayr-ee): The military is the armed forces of a country. Many people from Tennessee were in the military during the War of 1812.

museum (myoo-ZEE-um): A museum is a place where people go to see art, history, or science displays. The Country Music Hall of Fame and Museum is in Tennessee.

petals (PET-ulz): Petals are the colorful parts of flowers. The iris, Tennessee's state flower, often has purple petals.

popular (POP-yuh-lur): To be popular is to be enjoyed by many people. Country music is popular in Tennessee.

seal (SEEL): A seal is a symbol a state uses for government business. Tennessee's seal has plants and tools on it.

symbols (SIM-bulz): Symbols are pictures or things that stand for something else. The seal and the flag are Tennessee's symbols.

valleys (VAL-eez): Valleys are the low points between two mountains. Tennessee has valleys.

volunteer (vol-un-TEER): To volunteer means to do something without being asked or paid. Tennessee became known as "the Volunteer State" after the War of 1812.

Further Information

Books

Keller, Laurie. *The Scrambled States of America*. New York: Henry Holt, 2002.

Shoulders, Michael. *V is for Volunteer: A Tennessee Alphabet*. Chelsea, MI: Sleeping Bear Press, 2001.

Thornton, Brian. *The Everything Kids' States Book: Wind Your Way Across Our Great Nation*. Avon, MA: Adams Media, 2007.

Web Sites

Visit our Web site for links about Tennessee: *childsworld.com/links*

Note to Parents, Teachers, and Librarians: We routinely verify our Web links to make sure they are safe and active sites. So encourage your readers to check them out!

Index